PRINCEWILL LAGANG

Relationship Resilience: Weathering Life's Storms Together

First published by PRINCEWILL LAGANG 2023

Copyright © 2023 by Princewill Lagang

All rights reserved. No part of this publication may be reproduced, stored or transmitted in any form or by any means, electronic, mechanical, photocopying, recording, scanning, or otherwise without written permission from the publisher. It is illegal to copy this book, post it to a website, or distribute it by any other means without permission.

Princewill Lagang asserts the moral right to be identified as the author of this work.

First edition

This book was professionally typeset on Reedsy. Find out more at reedsy.com

Contents

1. Introduction to Relationship Resilience — 1
2. Building a Strong Foundation — 3
3. Communication Strategies for Resilience — 6
4. Navigating Conflict and Adversity — 9
5. Emotional Intimacy and Vulnerability — 12
6. Trust and Rebuilding After Setbacks — 15
7. Supporting Each Other's Growth — 18
8. Coping Together Through Life's Changes — 21
9. Parenting and Resilience as a Team — 24
10. Cultivating Joy and Positivity — 27
11. Seeking Outside Support When Needed — 30
12. The Ongoing Journey of Relationship Resilience — 33

1

Introduction to Relationship Resilience

In the realm of human connections, the intricate dance of relationships often encounters numerous challenges that test their strength and endurance. It is within these trials that the concept of relationship resilience emerges as a guiding light, illuminating the path for couples seeking to weather storms and emerge stronger. This chapter lays the foundation for our journey into the depths of relationship resilience, exploring its definition, significance, and the tantalizing promise it holds for those willing to engage in its pursuit.

Defining Relationship Resilience

Relationship resilience can be understood as the dynamic ability of a partnership to not only withstand adversity but to adapt, learn, and grow from it. In essence, it is the capacity of a relationship to bounce back from setbacks, nourishing the connection even when faced with the most formidable challenges. While resilience in an individual context often pertains to personal strength, in relationships, it takes on a collaborative dimension—a mutual, intertwined effort to navigate the ever-changing currents of life.

The Importance of Relationship Resilience

Why does relationship resilience matter? The answer lies in the inherent nature of human connections. Relationships, whether romantic or platonic, are integral to our emotional well-being. They provide a support system, a source of joy, and a mirror through which we understand ourselves. Yet, just as a ship encounters turbulent waters, relationships inevitably encounter rough patches. It is in these moments that relationship resilience shines. Couples with a high degree of resilience are better equipped to manage conflicts, communicate effectively, and maintain a sense of intimacy even in the face of challenges.

Setting the Stage for Exploration

As we embark on this journey through the intricacies of relationship resilience, we invite you to envision relationships as living entities, ones that demand nurturing, care, and a willingness to adapt. The chapters that follow will delve into the core components that contribute to relationship resilience: communication, empathy, conflict resolution, and self-care. We will explore strategies for cultivating these qualities, delving into real-life stories of couples who have triumphed over adversity, emerging not only unscathed but strengthened.

In an age where the pace of life often threatens to overwhelm even the most steadfast partnerships, the pursuit of relationship resilience takes on a profound significance. It promises a roadmap for couples to not only endure challenges but to flourish within them. The chapters ahead will provide tools, insights, and inspiration for forging a bond that not only stands the test of time but evolves and thrives through it.

So, with an open heart and a curious mind, let us delve into the world of relationship resilience—a world where love, commitment, and shared growth form the bedrock of enduring connections.

2

Building a Strong Foundation

In the journey towards relationship resilience, the importance of a solid foundation cannot be overstated. Just as a well-constructed house requires a sturdy base to withstand external forces, a resilient relationship thrives when built upon core elements that fortify its structure. This chapter delves into the essential components that lay the groundwork for a strong and lasting partnership, setting the stage for the development of relationship resilience.

Cultivating Trust and Open Communication

At the heart of any strong relationship lies trust—an unwavering belief in the reliability, honesty, and intentions of one another. Trust is the cornerstone upon which all other aspects of a relationship are built. It creates a safe space for vulnerability, essential for open communication. Effective communication, in turn, becomes the bridge connecting partners, allowing them to share their thoughts, feelings, and concerns openly and honestly.

Nurturing Emotional Intimacy

Emotional intimacy is the deep bond that emerges when partners share their innermost thoughts, fears, dreams, and desires. It's the ability to truly understand and empathize with each other's emotions. Nurturing emotional intimacy involves active listening, validating feelings, and creating an environment where both partners feel seen and heard.

Fostering Mutual Respect and Equality

Respect is the foundation of all healthy relationships. It involves recognizing each other's worth, acknowledging differences, and treating one another with kindness and consideration. In a resilient partnership, respect extends to maintaining a sense of equality, where decisions are made collaboratively, and power dynamics are balanced.

Embracing Flexibility and Adaptability

Life is unpredictable, and challenges are inevitable. Resilient relationships are characterized by their ability to adapt to changing circumstances. Flexibility means being open to compromise, finding solutions together, and adjusting expectations when necessary. Partners who embrace flexibility can navigate obstacles with greater ease and maintain their connection even during times of change.

Cultivating Shared Goals and Values

Partnerships that share common goals and values have a stronger sense of purpose. These shared aspirations create a roadmap for the relationship, giving it direction and meaning. Whether it's building a family, pursuing career goals, or exploring new experiences, aligning on fundamental values helps couples navigate decisions and challenges with a sense of unity.

Prioritizing Quality Time and Individual Growth

Spending quality time together is essential for maintaining a strong bond. It's not just about being physically present; it's about engaging in activities that foster connection and create cherished memories. At the same time, allowing each other space for individual growth and pursuing personal interests enriches the relationship by bringing new experiences and perspectives to the partnership.

Conclusion

The process of building a strong foundation in a relationship is akin to crafting a masterpiece—a delicate balance of trust, communication, intimacy, respect, flexibility, shared goals, and personal growth. These elements work harmoniously to create a resilient partnership that not only withstands the tests of time but thrives in the face of adversity. As we move forward in our exploration of relationship resilience, remember that the effort invested in building a strong foundation lays the groundwork for the transformative journey ahead.

3

Communication Strategies for Resilience

Effective communication serves as the lifeblood of any resilient relationship. It acts as a bridge that connects partners, enabling them to navigate challenges, resolve conflicts, and deepen their connection. This chapter delves into the crucial role of communication in building relationship resilience and offers strategies for fostering open dialogue, active listening, and mutual understanding.

The Vital Role of Effective Communication

Communication acts as the compass that guides couples through the intricate landscape of their partnership. It is the means by which they express emotions, share experiences, and address issues. Healthy communication is essential because it promotes understanding, reduces misunderstandings, and helps partners feel valued and validated.

Open Dialogue: Creating a Safe Space

Creating an environment of open dialogue encourages partners to share their thoughts and feelings freely. To do this, both individuals must feel safe and comfortable expressing themselves without fear of judgment or criticism. Establishing ground rules for communication, such as avoiding blame and practicing empathy, sets the stage for productive conversations.

Active Listening: Hearing and Understanding

Active listening is a foundational skill in effective communication. It involves not just hearing the words spoken by a partner, but also understanding the underlying emotions and intentions. Partners should practice giving their full attention, maintaining eye contact, and asking clarifying questions to ensure that they comprehend each other's perspectives accurately.

Empathy: Walking in Each Other's Shoes

Empathy is the ability to understand and share the feelings of another person. It is a powerful tool for building connection and resolving conflicts. By genuinely trying to see the world from the other person's perspective, partners can create a deeper bond and demonstrate that they value each other's emotions.

Nonviolent Communication: Expressing Without Harming

Nonviolent communication (NVC) is an approach that focuses on expressing oneself without causing harm or defensiveness in the listener. It involves using "I" statements to convey feelings and needs, rather than blaming or accusing. NVC promotes active listening and fosters an atmosphere of mutual respect and understanding.

Constructive Conflict Resolution: Turning Challenges into Growth

Conflict is a natural part of any relationship, but how it is handled can make or break a partnership. Constructive conflict resolution involves addressing differences with the intention of finding solutions rather than assigning blame. Partners can use techniques such as "time-outs" to cool off during heated discussions, focusing on the issue rather than personal attacks, and seeking compromise.

Digital Communication Etiquette: Navigating the Modern Landscape

In the digital age, communication extends beyond face-to-face interactions. Partners must be mindful of how they communicate through text, social media, and other digital platforms. Clear and respectful digital communication is just as important for maintaining a strong foundation.

Conclusion

Communication is the heartbeat of a resilient relationship, pulsating with the rhythms of understanding, empathy, and shared experiences. By fostering open dialogue, practicing active listening, and embracing techniques for empathy and conflict resolution, partners can create a rich tapestry of connection that weathers storms and emerges stronger. As we move forward in our exploration of relationship resilience, remember that the art of communication is not just about talking—it's about truly hearing, understanding, and nurturing the profound connection that lies at the core of every enduring partnership.

4

Navigating Conflict and Adversity

In the intricate web of relationships, conflicts and adversities are inevitable. However, it is how partners navigate these challenges that defines the resilience of their bond. This chapter explores approaches to handling conflicts and adversity constructively, while preserving respect, understanding, and connection.

Understanding Conflict as an Opportunity

Conflicts are not necessarily destructive; they can serve as catalysts for growth and understanding. Viewing conflicts as opportunities for learning allows partners to approach them with a positive mindset, seeking solutions that lead to mutual understanding and personal development.

Effective Communication in Conflict Resolution

During conflicts, communication becomes even more crucial. Partners should approach discussions with a commitment to active listening and expressing their thoughts and emotions constructively. Avoiding blame and focusing on the issue at hand rather than personal attacks are essential principles for effective communication.

Respectful Disagreement: Maintaining Mutual Regard

Disagreements don't have to lead to disrespect or hurtful exchanges. It's possible to disagree while still maintaining a sense of mutual regard. Partners can express their differing opinions respectfully, acknowledging that differences are a natural part of any relationship.

Seeking Common Ground: Collaboration over Competition

Conflict resolution is not about "winning" an argument, but rather finding common ground through collaboration. Partners should work together to identify shared goals and compromise where needed. This approach fosters a sense of unity and teamwork, reinforcing the strength of the relationship.

Embracing Empathy During Adversity

Adversity, whether external challenges or internal struggles, calls for heightened empathy. Partners should seek to understand each other's feelings and perspectives, offering support and comfort. This shared empathy strengthens the emotional bond and reminds both individuals that they are not alone in their journey.

Managing Stress: A Unified Front

External stressors can strain a relationship. Partners can proactively manage stress by communicating their concerns, offering reassurance, and finding ways to support each other. Approaching challenges as a unified front rather than as adversaries bolsters the relationship's resilience.

Time and Space: The Power of Patience

In moments of conflict and adversity, emotions can run high. Taking time and space to cool off can prevent impulsive reactions and provide the opportunity for rational thinking. Agreeing on a "time-out" mechanism and setting boundaries for respectful communication during these breaks can be beneficial.

Conclusion

Navigating conflict and adversity requires a delicate balance of patience, communication, and empathy. Partners who approach challenges as opportunities for growth, maintain respect during disagreements, and stand united in the face of adversity are better equipped to weather life's storms. As we delve further into the realm of relationship resilience, remember that the way a couple handles conflicts and adversities speaks volumes about the strength of their connection—transforming challenges into stepping stones towards a deeper, more profound bond.

5

Emotional Intimacy and Vulnerability

At the heart of every resilient relationship lies emotional intimacy—a profound connection that thrives when partners willingly embrace vulnerability and authenticity. This chapter delves into the pivotal role of emotional intimacy in relationship resilience and offers techniques for deepening emotional bonds and fostering vulnerability.

Emotional Intimacy: The Foundation of Resilience

Emotional intimacy is the cornerstone upon which relationship resilience is built. It involves sharing one's deepest thoughts, feelings, fears, and aspirations with a partner. This level of vulnerability creates a safe space for mutual understanding and empathy, allowing partners to weather challenges with a sense of unity.

Creating a Culture of Emotional Safety

To foster emotional intimacy, partners must establish a culture of emotional safety. This means creating an environment where both individuals feel comfortable expressing their emotions without fear of judgment or rejection.

Respect, active listening, and nonviolent communication are key components of this environment.

Embracing Vulnerability: Strength in Openness

Vulnerability is often misunderstood as weakness, but in truth, it is an immense source of strength. Being vulnerable means letting down one's guard and allowing a partner to see the unfiltered, authentic self. This openness invites reciprocity, deepening the emotional connection.

Building Trust: The Bridge to Vulnerability

Trust is the bridge that leads to vulnerability. Partners must trust that their vulnerabilities will be met with compassion and understanding. As trust grows, the willingness to share becomes more natural, further solidifying the emotional bond.

Emotional Expressiveness: Cultivating Open Communication

Expressing emotions openly is vital for emotional intimacy. Partners can practice sharing their feelings regularly, whether it's joy, sadness, frustration, or excitement. Encouraging and supporting each other's emotional expressiveness nurtures a deeper understanding of each other's inner worlds.

Creating Rituals of Connection: Nurturing Togetherness

Rituals of connection are shared activities that partners engage in regularly to strengthen their bond. These can be as simple as enjoying a cup of coffee together in the morning or setting aside time for a weekly date night. These rituals create opportunities for emotional intimacy to flourish.

Active Empathy: Walking in Each Other's Emotional Shoes

Empathy goes beyond understanding; it's about feeling what the other person feels. Active empathy involves tuning into a partner's emotions and demonstrating that their feelings matter. Partners can validate emotions by saying, "I can see why you feel that way" or "I understand why that's important to you."

Conclusion

Emotional intimacy and vulnerability are the threads that weave together the fabric of a resilient relationship. Partners who willingly share their innermost selves, embrace vulnerability, and create an environment of emotional safety forge a connection that endures challenges and flourishes through time. As we continue our exploration of relationship resilience, remember that it's in the vulnerability of sharing one's heart that the true strength of a partnership is revealed—an unbreakable bond that stands strong even in the face of life's greatest tests.

6

Trust and Rebuilding After Setbacks

Trust is the bedrock upon which resilient relationships are built. It's the delicate fabric that holds partners together during times of adversity and strengthens their connection. This chapter delves into the significance of trust in relationship resilience and offers strategies for rebuilding trust after challenges or breaches.

The Essence of Trust in Resilient Relationships

Trust is the glue that binds partners together through thick and thin. It's the unwavering belief that a partner's intentions and actions are aligned with the well-being of the relationship. Trust provides a sense of security, allowing partners to be vulnerable, express themselves openly, and confront challenges with a united front.

Understanding Trust Erosion: Causes and Consequences

Trust can be eroded due to various factors, such as dishonesty, broken promises, or breaches of boundaries. When trust is compromised, partners may experience feelings of betrayal, hurt, and insecurity. Rebuilding trust becomes paramount to restoring the relationship's resilience.

Open Communication: Addressing Trust Issues

When trust is shaken, partners must engage in open and honest communication. Discussing the reasons for the breach of trust, sharing feelings, and acknowledging the impact of the incident is a crucial step. Partners should express remorse and a commitment to rebuilding trust moving forward.

Consistency and Reliability: The Foundation of Rebuilding Trust

Rebuilding trust requires consistent and reliable behavior. Partners must demonstrate that their words and actions align, and they are committed to upholding the promises they make. Over time, consistent behavior helps rebuild a sense of predictability and reliability.

Transparency: A Window to Rebuilding Trust

Transparency involves sharing information openly and honestly, especially when it relates to the incident that caused trust to be compromised. Partners can demonstrate transparency by willingly sharing their thoughts, feelings, and actions, even if it feels uncomfortable.

Setting Boundaries: Preventing Future Trust Breaches

As partners work to rebuild trust, setting clear boundaries becomes essential. Both individuals should openly discuss what is acceptable behavior and what is not. Setting and respecting boundaries ensures that the relationship remains a safe space for both partners.

Forgiveness and Healing: The Road to Renewal

Forgiveness is a pivotal step in rebuilding trust. It involves letting go of the pain and resentment caused by the breach and choosing to move forward. Forgiveness doesn't mean forgetting; rather, it's a conscious decision to release the emotional burden.

Conclusion

Trust, once broken, can be rebuilt with patience, effort, and a genuine desire to restore the bond. Partners who address trust issues through open communication, consistent behavior, transparency, and forgiveness can mend the fabric of their relationship and emerge even stronger. As we continue our exploration of relationship resilience, remember that trust is the pillar that supports the bridge between partners, allowing them to cross tumultuous waters together, hand in hand.

7

Supporting Each Other's Growth

In the intricate dance of relationships, the pursuit of individual growth can sometimes feel at odds with the goal of maintaining a strong partnership. However, the truth is that supporting each other's personal aspirations can significantly contribute to relationship resilience. This chapter explores the delicate balance of nurturing individual growth within the context of a partnership and how doing so strengthens the bond between partners.

Recognizing the Importance of Individual Growth

Healthy relationships are not about two people merging into one; they are about two individuals coming together to enhance each other's lives. Nurturing individual growth acknowledges that each partner has unique dreams, goals, and desires that contribute to their sense of self and overall well-being.

Balancing Individual Aspirations and Shared Goals

Supporting each other's growth doesn't mean neglecting the relationship's shared goals. Rather, it's about finding a balance between pursuing personal aspirations and nurturing the connection. Partners can encourage each other to pursue their passions while ensuring that the relationship remains a priority.

Fostering Independence and Autonomy

Maintaining a sense of independence within the relationship is essential for individual growth. Partners should feel comfortable pursuing their interests, spending time with friends and family, and engaging in activities that bring them joy. This autonomy enriches the relationship by infusing it with diverse experiences and perspectives.

Active Support and Encouragement

Partners who actively support each other's growth provide a solid foundation for resilience. They celebrate achievements, no matter how small, and offer encouragement during moments of self-doubt. This support reinforces the idea that both individuals are invested in each other's success and happiness.

Communication about Goals and Aspirations

Clear and open communication is key to supporting each other's growth. Partners should discuss their goals, dreams, and aspirations openly, sharing what matters most to them. Regular check-ins allow them to provide guidance, celebrate progress, and make adjustments as needed.

Creating a Growth-Friendly Environment

A growth-friendly environment is one where partners feel safe to express their ambitions without fear of judgment. Encouragement, active listening, and shared enthusiasm for each other's goals cultivate a space that nurtures individual growth.

Shared Learning and Experiences

Partners can actively engage in each other's growth by participating in shared learning experiences. Whether it's attending a workshop, exploring a new hobby, or attending each other's events, these shared moments not only enrich the partnership but also contribute to the individual's growth.

Conclusion

Supporting each other's growth is a dynamic dance of fostering independence while nurturing the connection. Partners who champion each other's aspirations, communicate openly, and actively engage in the journey of personal development strengthen the resilience of their relationship. As we venture further into the realm of relationship resilience, remember that a partnership thrives not just when it is a source of stability, but when it acts as a catalyst for each partner's growth—a beautiful intertwining of individual flourishing and shared strength.

8

Coping Together Through Life's Changes

Life is a journey marked by an ever-changing landscape of transitions—some anticipated, others unexpected. These shifts can deeply affect relationship resilience, as partners navigate new challenges and uncertainties together. This chapter explores the impact of life transitions on relationships and offers strategies for adapting and supporting each other through change.

Understanding the Impact of Life Transitions

Life transitions, whether positive or challenging, can significantly impact relationship dynamics. They may include events like career changes, moving to a new place, becoming parents, facing health issues, or dealing with loss. Transitions can disrupt routines, alter roles, and evoke strong emotions, all of which can test the resilience of a relationship.

Recognizing Individual Responses to Change

Each partner may respond differently to a life transition based on their personality, experiences, and coping mechanisms. Some individuals may embrace change eagerly, while others might feel anxious or resistant. Understanding these differences and respecting each other's unique reactions is essential for maintaining a strong bond.

Strengthening the Partnership through Communication

Effective communication is crucial during times of change. Partners should openly discuss their feelings, concerns, and expectations related to the transition. Sharing hopes and fears creates an environment of mutual support and reinforces the idea that both individuals are in this together.

Flexibility and Adaptability: Navigating the Unknown

Transitions often bring the unknown into focus. Partners can navigate this uncertainty by embracing flexibility and adaptability. Being open to adjusting plans, setting realistic expectations, and focusing on the journey rather than the destination help partners navigate change with greater ease.

Shared Decision-Making: Unity in Choices

During transitions, decisions may need to be made that impact both partners. Engaging in shared decision-making, where both individuals contribute their thoughts and preferences, creates a sense of unity. It's important to prioritize compromise and collaboration to ensure that choices reflect the needs of both partners.

Providing Emotional Support

Transitions can be emotionally taxing. Partners should actively provide emotional support by listening empathetically, offering reassurance, and validating each other's feelings. Expressing love and commitment during moments of vulnerability reinforces the resilience of the relationship.

Maintaining Rituals and Routines

Amidst change, maintaining familiar rituals and routines can provide a sense of stability. Shared activities, whether it's cooking dinner together or going for a regular walk, offer a comforting anchor during times of flux.

Conclusion

Life's transitions are a testament to the ebb and flow of existence. Partners who navigate these changes hand in hand, acknowledging individual responses, communicating openly, and embracing adaptability, build a relationship that thrives through every twist and turn. As we delve deeper into the exploration of relationship resilience, remember that it's during life's transitions that the true strength of a partnership is unveiled—a partnership that evolves, adapts, and emerges even more resilient than before.

9

Parenting and Resilience as a Team

The journey of parenthood is a remarkable chapter in a relationship—one that brings immense joy and new challenges. Navigating the complexities of parenting while maintaining a resilient bond requires teamwork, communication, and adaptability. This chapter explores approaches to co-parenting that foster resilience and strategies for maintaining a strong connection amidst the demands of parenting.

Co-Parenting as a Shared Endeavor

Co-parenting is a joint endeavor that demands collaboration and mutual support. Partners must approach parenting decisions as a team, respecting each other's opinions and working together to provide a nurturing environment for their children.

Clear Communication: The Foundation of Co-Parenting

Open and clear communication is paramount in co-parenting. Partners should discuss parenting styles, expectations, and values to ensure they are on the same page. Regular check-ins allow adjustments and prevent misunderstandings.

Balancing Roles and Responsibilities

Balancing the demands of parenting with personal and shared responsibilities is essential. Partners should work together to distribute tasks fairly, allowing both individuals to maintain their sense of self while contributing to the family unit.

Quality Time as a Couple

Parenting can be all-consuming, but partners should strive to maintain quality time as a couple. Regular date nights, moments of connection, and shared hobbies help keep the romantic bond alive amidst the busyness of parenting.

Supporting Each Other's Parenting Roles

Each partner brings unique strengths to parenting. Acknowledging and supporting these strengths fosters a sense of unity and allows children to benefit from a diverse range of experiences.

Navigating Challenges with Unity

Parenting inevitably presents challenges. Partners should approach these challenges as a united front, working together to find solutions. It's important to avoid undermining each other's authority and to address disagreements privately.

Prioritizing Self-Care and Connection

Parenting can be draining, making self-care and maintaining the couple's connection crucial. Partners should encourage each other to engage in activities that rejuvenate them and prioritize moments of intimacy.

Creating a Supportive Network

Building a supportive network of family, friends, and other parents can alleviate some of the challenges of parenting. Seeking advice, sharing experiences, and receiving help when needed strengthen the partnership and the family unit.

Conclusion

Co-parenting is a shared journey that requires dedication, patience, and a commitment to communication. Partners who approach parenting as a team, navigate challenges with unity, and prioritize both their children's well-being and their relationship's resilience create a harmonious balance that benefits the entire family. As we continue our exploration of relationship resilience, remember that parenting is a chapter in a larger story—a story of a partnership that evolves and endures through the joys and challenges of nurturing a family.

10

Cultivating Joy and Positivity

In the intricate tapestry of relationships, the threads of joy and positivity play a crucial role in building resilience. Infusing a partnership with a sense of optimism and gratitude enhances its ability to weather challenges and flourish. This chapter explores the significance of positivity in relationship resilience and offers techniques for finding joy and gratitude in daily life.

The Power of Positivity in Resilient Relationships

Positivity acts as a protective shield, buffering relationships from the strains of adversity. Partners who cultivate joy and maintain a positive outlook are better equipped to face challenges, communicate effectively, and adapt to life's changes. Positivity enhances resilience by fostering emotional connection, promoting problem-solving, and encouraging mutual support.

Embracing the Practice of Gratitude

Gratitude is a transformative practice that shifts focus from what's lacking to what's abundant. Partners who practice gratitude express appreciation for each other's efforts, acknowledge the blessings in their lives, and cultivate a sense of contentment.

Finding Joy in the Everyday Moments

Amidst the demands of life, finding joy in everyday moments nourishes the relationship. Partners can engage in activities they both enjoy, embark on new adventures, or simply savor the simple pleasures of life together.

Positive Communication: The Language of Resilience

Positive communication involves framing discussions in an optimistic light. Instead of dwelling on problems, partners can focus on solutions, strengths, and potential growth. This approach fosters a sense of teamwork and collaboration.

Humor as a Bonding Agent

Humor has the remarkable ability to lighten heavy moments and create shared laughter. Partners who share inside jokes, playful banter, and lighthearted moments strengthen their emotional connection and infuse the relationship with joy.

Mindfulness: Being Present Together

Practicing mindfulness involves being fully present in the moment. Partners can engage in mindfulness activities such as deep breathing, meditation, or enjoying nature together. This shared presence deepens the connection and helps partners appreciate each other and life's beauty.

Spreading Positivity: Acts of Kindness

Small acts of kindness and thoughtfulness amplify positivity in a relationship.

Partners can surprise each other with gestures that show they are thinking of each other, whether it's a heartfelt note, a favorite meal, or a simple compliment.

Creating a Positive Environment

Partners can actively create an environment that promotes positivity by surrounding themselves with uplifting influences, whether it's through music, art, literature, or spending time in nature. A positive environment nourishes the emotional well-being of both individuals.

Conclusion

Cultivating joy and positivity in a relationship is akin to tending a garden that yields vibrant blossoms even in the harshest weather. Partners who embrace positivity, practice gratitude, and find joy in everyday moments create a resilient partnership that thrives through both sunshine and rain. As we conclude our exploration of relationship resilience, remember that the energy of positivity is a gift that partners can give to each other, nurturing a bond that not only endures but radiates with the warmth of shared joy.

11

Seeking Outside Support When Needed

In the journey of relationship resilience, there are times when the challenges become overwhelming and the tools at hand may not be sufficient. Seeking outside support, whether from professionals or support networks, can be a transformative step that strengthens the bond between partners. This chapter delves into recognizing when to seek help and how external resources can enhance relationship resilience.

Recognizing Signs for Seeking Help

Recognizing the signs that outside support is needed is a crucial skill in relationship resilience. These signs may include persistent conflicts, communication breakdowns, emotional distancing, or challenges that impact overall well-being. If partners find themselves struggling to find solutions, it's a clear indicator that seeking outside help could be beneficial.

Professional Guidance: A Path to Healing

Professional guidance, such as couples therapy or counseling, offers a structured space for partners to explore their challenges with the guidance of a trained therapist. Therapists provide tools, strategies, and insights that help partners navigate difficulties, communicate effectively, and rebuild trust.

Support Networks: The Power of Community

Engaging with support networks, whether friends, family, or peer groups, offers partners an external perspective and a sense of belonging. Sharing experiences, seeking advice, and receiving encouragement from those who care can provide a much-needed boost during challenging times.

Learning from Others: Role Models of Resilience

Role models who have successfully navigated challenges and built resilient relationships can serve as inspiration. Learning from their experiences and seeking their advice can provide valuable insights into maintaining a strong bond.

Education and Resources: Strengthening Resilience Skills

Engaging in workshops, reading books, or attending seminars on relationship resilience can equip partners with practical tools and strategies. These resources provide a framework for nurturing the partnership and building a foundation of strength.

Maintaining Openness to Outside Help

Cultivating a willingness to seek outside help requires humility and open-mindedness. Partners should recognize that asking for help is a sign of strength, not weakness. It demonstrates the commitment to the relationship's well-being and growth.

Regular Check-Ins and Tune-Ups

Even in the absence of major challenges, seeking outside support for regular check-ins or tune-ups can be beneficial. Preventive measures, such as attending relationship workshops or scheduling periodic therapy sessions, ensure that the relationship remains strong and resilient.

Conclusion

Recognizing when to seek outside support is an integral part of relationship resilience. Whether through professional guidance, support networks, or learning from others, external resources provide partners with fresh perspectives, tools, and insights to navigate challenges and nurture their bond. As we conclude our exploration of relationship resilience, remember that seeking help is not a sign of weakness, but a testament to the dedication partners have towards nurturing a partnership that stands strong even in the face of life's most formidable tests.

12

The Ongoing Journey of Relationship Resilience

As we draw near to the end of our exploration, it's essential to reflect on the ongoing journey of building and maintaining relationship resilience. Resilience is not a destination but a continuous practice that requires dedication, effort, and a commitment to growth. This final chapter delves into the significance of nurturing a culture of resilience as an enduring act of love.

Embracing the Evolution of Resilience

Resilience is not a fixed state but an evolving process. Partners must understand that challenges will arise, and their bond will be tested. However, the growth that occurs through these challenges is what strengthens the relationship over time.

Reflecting on the Journey

Taking moments to reflect on the journey of relationship resilience allows partners to appreciate how far they've come. Reflecting on the challenges they've overcome and the growth they've experienced reinforces their shared commitment and deepens their bond.

Adapting and Learning

The journey of resilience is marked by adaptation and learning. Partners should be open to learning from each other, from external resources, and from their own experiences. Adaptation is a sign of flexibility and willingness to evolve together.

Perseverance through Trials

Trials and tribulations are an inevitable part of life. Partners who persevere through challenges with a sense of unity and determination reinforce their resilience. Remember that every trial you overcome strengthens the foundation of your relationship.

Nurturing a Culture of Resilience

Building a culture of resilience involves creating an environment where both partners actively contribute to the relationship's growth and well-being. This culture is fostered through effective communication, support, respect, and a commitment to finding joy even during difficult times.

Cherishing Moments of Connection

Amidst the hustle and bustle of life, it's important to cherish moments of connection. Partners can engage in activities that strengthen their bond, express appreciation for each other, and create lasting memories.

Cultivating an Attitude of Gratitude

Practicing gratitude is a cornerstone of relationship resilience. Partners can actively express appreciation for each other's efforts, remind themselves of the blessings they share, and cultivate an attitude of thankfulness.

Continuing the Journey of Love

Ultimately, the journey of relationship resilience is a journey of love. Partners who actively work on nurturing their connection, supporting each other, and adapting to life's changes demonstrate a profound love that evolves, endures, and flourishes.

Conclusion

As we conclude this exploration of relationship resilience, remember that the journey doesn't end here—it continues with every choice, every act of kindness, and every shared moment. Building and maintaining resilience is not just about overcoming challenges; it's about the love and dedication partners have for each other. As you move forward, may you continue to nurture your partnership, embrace growth, and celebrate the ongoing journey of love and resilience.

Summary: Relationship Resilience—Weathering Life's Storms Together

In the intricate tapestry of life, relationships stand as some of our most precious threads. They are the bonds that offer us companionship, support, and a sense of belonging. But just as the weather can change, so can the circumstances that challenge these bonds. Through the pages of this exploration, we've delved into the art of relationship resilience—a journey that equips partners with the tools, strategies, and mindset to weather life's storms together.

From defining the essence of relationship resilience to cultivating emotional intimacy, supporting each other's growth, and seeking outside help when needed, we've uncovered the intricate pathways that lead to a stronger, more enduring connection. We've discovered that resilience isn't just about surviving hardships—it's about thriving through them, emerging with a bond that's deeper, more profound, and capable of withstanding the tests of time.

Relationship resilience is a symphony of efforts: the harmonious notes of effective communication, the melodies of shared joy, the rhythm of embracing vulnerability, and the crescendo of unwavering support. It's a continuous journey of learning, adapting, and growing—a journey that requires dedication, patience, and the profound willingness to stand side by side as partners in love and life.

As you venture forward on your own paths of resilience, remember that challenges are not obstacles but stepping stones. Each test you face, each storm you weather, is an opportunity for growth, understanding, and renewal. Just as a tree's roots dig deep to anchor it during turbulent winds, so too can your relationship's resilience ground you and guide you through the ever-changing landscape.

Relationship resilience is a testament to the power of love—the love that drives you to communicate openly, to embrace vulnerability, to celebrate joy, and to support each other's dreams. It's the love that compels you to seek help when needed, to adapt to life's changes, and to find strength in unity. This journey is not without its challenges, but it's within those challenges that the true essence of your partnership is revealed—a partnership that stands resilient, unwavering, and forever entwined.

As you continue your own voyage of relationship resilience, may you find the strength to embrace the storms, the wisdom to adapt, and the love to hold each other close, always. Through the highs and lows, through the joys and sorrows, may your journey be one of growth, connection, and an unbreakable bond that endures through every season of life.

www.ingramcontent.com/pod-product-compliance
Lightning Source LLC
LaVergne TN
LVHW010441070526
838199LV00066B/6117